KEYSTONE
BANGVILLE POLICE
FARCE COMEDY
KEYSTONE FILM COMPANY
NEW YORK

Columbia Pictures Corp
presents
HERE COMES Mr. JORDAN
Copyright mcmxli by Columbia

THE TALL GUY

THE MAN WHO LAUGHS
A PAUL LENI PRODUCTION

THE TALL GUY

The Awful Truth
COPYRIGHT MCMXXXVII BY COLUMBIA PICTURES CORP OF CALIF LTD.
HARRY COHN, PRESIDENT

THE MAN WITHOUT A BODY

COPS

COLUMBIA PICTURES CORPORATION
PRESENTS THE
MAN WHO TURNED TO STONE
COPYRIGHT © MCMLVII BY COLUMBIA PICTURES CORPORATION
ALL RIGHTS RESERVED

THE MAN WITHOUT A BODY

40010
THE ANGRY SILENCE

Gordon Jones
and
Joyce Compton
in
"POLICE ROOKIE"

THE DARK KNIGHT

GH⚬ST BUSTERS

"SHADOWS"
PRODUCED BY
PREFERRED PICTURES INC.
DISTRIBUTED BY
AL LICHTMAN CORPORATION

in
Ghosts on the Loose
Co-starring
BELA LUGOSI
COPYRIGHT MCMXLIII by MONOGRAM PICTURES CORP.

ALL NIGHT LONG

HEAVENS ABOVE !
© 1963 CHARTER FILM PRODUCTIONS LTD.

Metro-Goldwyn-Mayer
PRESENTS
HELEN HAYES and ROBERT MONTGOMERY
in
ANOTHER LANGUAGE

BLOOD

A*P*E

HAL ROACH
Presents
"THE DEVIL
WITH HITLER"
Released through
UNITED ARTISTS
COPYRIGHT MCMXLII BY HAL ROACH STUDIOS, INC.

SCREAM

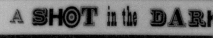

A SHOT in the DARK

OUT OF THE BLUE

GIANT

ZOMBIE

RADIO PICTURES
PRESENTS
BEHIND OFFICE DOORS
BY ALAN BRENER SCHULTZ
WITH
MARY ASTOR · ROBERT AMES
RICARDO CORTEZ
DIRECTED BY
MELVILLE BROWN
PRODUCED BY WILLIAM LEBARON

LETHAL WEAPON

Metro-Goldwyn-Mayer
Presents
"Eyes In The Night"
COPYRIGHT MCMLIV IN U.S.A.
BY LOEW'S INCORPORATED

THE BLACK HOLE

IT'S
THE
RAGE

BLOODLUST!

Producers Releasing Corporation
PRESENTS
THE MAD
MONSTER

SABRINA
COPYRIGHT MEMLIV BY PARAMOUNT PICTURES CORPORATION
ALL RIGHTS RESERVED
Paramount Pictures Corporation

HOSTAGE

in
'HIS KIND OF WOMAN'
A
JOHN FARROW PRODUCTION
COPYRIGHT MCMLI RKO RADIO PICTURES, INC.
ALL RIGHTS RESERVED

RADIO PICTURES
PRESENTS
H. RIDER HAGGARD'S
SHE
A MERIAN C. COOPER PRODUCTION

Columbia Pictures Corporation
PRESENTS
Not a Ladies' Man
PAUL
KELLY   FAY
WRAY   Douglass
CROFT

Hello,
Dolly!

I EAT YOUR SKIN
A CINEMATION INDUSTRIES, INC. RELEASE

Plaudit Productions presents
"Aroused"

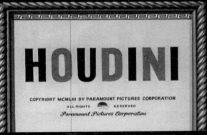

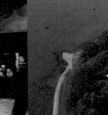

STARTLE

TORSTEN LAUSCHMANN

DUNDEE CONTEMPORARY ARTS
FILM AND VIDEO UMBRELLA

PHANTASMAGORIA

Movement and stillness are the constituents of visual culture: movements turned into still images in sequential photography; still images sequenced together to provide the illusion of movement or to reconstitute a movement from the past. The transitions between movement and stillness are unseen by the human eye, in the case of the cinematic strip rushing through the projector. But, in other instances, visual culture dramatises the transitions between movement and stillness. It can be a part of the act. When the first films were shown on the first screens, they began not with images of movement, but rather stasis. On the screen, before the audience, a still image was suddenly cranked into life and the coil of filmstrip rushed through the projector until its end. The delight derived not from the scene on the screen alone, but from viewing the transition from stillness to movement, or, in other words, witnessing the actual event of the inputting of quasi-life. The moment was magic. Animation is movement impelled not internally, by the mover, but through some sort of external force: the hand spinning the wheel, the lantern slides manipulated by an operator, the frames rushed at the right speed through the projector. Animation dramatises the leap into movement from stillness and so retains the moment of wonder and delight: that something like life can be bestowed. Of course, that transition between stillness and movement, that magical moment, is more readily accessed in the device that is spun by hand and then comes to rest, or in the small strip that loops and in returning to the start again, at least unconsciously, indicates an ending, a stopping that is cranked again into starting. Film, with its narrative development and lack of looping that parallels the self-impelled movement of actual life, lessens this effect.

By the time of the first films, audiences were used to the mobilisation of stillness into movement, before their very eyes.

Magic lantern shows, which enjoyed a highpoint in London in the 1860s, conjured up different types of movement out of stillness. Two or more glass slides were manipulated so that dissolves and swoops, changes of scale or colour seamlessly occurred. Fishes swim. Skeletons appear and disappear. A rat attacks a man. Flowers blossom, acrobats twirl – anything and everything happens, the more colourful the better. Thrill was solicited in these little loops of jerky movement. In the megalethoscopes of the 1870s, movement is not in the object depicted, but rather the movement of celestial bodies. Day is exchanged for night, as lighting effects stream over a translucent and pierced scene of a church, a palace, a pyramid. Night gives way to day, as the loop of nature is emulated. The nineteenth century entertainments stoked the delights of time passing, or at least circling, and of stillness impelled into movement, even if that movement was looped.

The magic lantern, in its hundreds of years of existence, proliferated into various devices, some of which took on the suffix 'scope', some the suffix 'rama'. In the late eighteenth century, a more enveloping optical entertainment developed when a magic lantern was incorporated into a theatrical environment. It was named the Phantasmagoria, and within this display the magic lantern was more usually turned to the dark side. Scary prospects were projected, swiftly changing in size and gifted with great mobility. The contorting ghouls and devils were designed to terrify the viewers and root them to the spot, immobilised in awe. Such optical displays developed a set of movements that were later taken up into film camerawork: the 'zoom', 'dissolve', the 'tracking-shot' and superimposition. Mobility is a quality of the machinery that projects (in conjunction with its operator) and, later, of the device that records (in conjunction with its operator).

Phantasmagoria is a word used in a social, political and economic context by Karl Marx, in his presentation of commodity fetishism and its secrets in the first volume of *Capital*, published in 1867. As historical, technical artifact, the phantasmagoria is a magic lantern that made brightly coloured images move and twirl. The images of things seemingly come alive often showing, conversely, dead things, like ghosts and skeletons, in order to incite shudder, shock and wonder. Marx ascribes the phantasmagoric vision to a social moment of production. Phantasmagoric is how he characterises the illusory relationship between humans and the commodities that they have produced within a capitalist market system. Workers make the commodities, yet these marketable objects seem to rule over their makers. They become animated. The products are dead but seem more alive than their producers, who cower in the darkness of the factory system. Commodities in the market possess a liveliness – corn rises, silver falls, iron jumps. Humans, on the other hand, are subordinated to these apparently miraculous value-generating things, and are described sometimes in abstract terms as just a hand – 'hands required'. Movement is a quality of the thing. Impelled movement – being an appendage of the machine – is a quality of the person. A social relation between people, notes Marx, assumes, in their own eyes, the phantasmagoric form of a relation between things. Things communicate with other things, their worth pitched as more or less than that of each other. The value of their makers is only a matter for calculation in relation to wages, a mathematical sum carried on in relation to their labour power as commodity. In all this, the commodity appears as animated by its own accord, an objective being, not the result of human and collective labour. Marx compares the process to the misty productions of religion – Gods invented by man are said to have invented man. The 'phantasmagoric' comes to denote a flawed vision, socially and historically achieved, and is, for Marx, a deceptive one. But it is also a contradictory vision: it takes the ghostly commodity shell for substance; human labour is occluded by a fantasy of self-generation; the dead thing is taken to be a lively entity. The optical entertainment known as the phantasmagoria stages contradictions too: light is used to produce dark images; substantial presence is suggested, when it is, in fact, only illusion; what seems to be self-motivated movement is actually manipulated more or less invisibly.

Walter Benjamin adopts the idea of the phantasmagoria of commodity capitalism in his writings on nineteenth-century Paris. In that 'city of mirrors' there are staged, in a variety of ways, confrontations of appearance and reality, a dreamy melding of reality and illusion. It occurs in the world exhibitions, the arcades, the department stores, in advertising, in the interior, the boulevards. Phantasmagoria for Benjamin, as for Marx, is a name for the curious mobility, activity, animation, and luminosity of the commodity. In an addendum to his piece *Paris of the Second Empire in Baudelaire*, Benjamin writes about taste as a faux-expertise that arises in the late nineteenth century, the further the consumer gets from knowledge about the technical and social production of goods. The exercise of taste masks the lack of knowledge in the consumer and acts as a stimulus for buying, benefiting the manufacturer. Taste – the ability to see at a glance the attractive aspects of a commodity that make it worth buying, as opposed to all the other similar looking ones – relies on an eye-catching surface, on the appearance of a commodity, on its dramatic appeal to the potential consumer. Benjamin describes this commodity surface as a gleam, a shimmer (Schein) that phosphoresces. It draws the eye. The commodity appears to be a type of optical entertainment in itself. In the commodity caves of the cities, the phosphorescent commodities distract and seduce. Today the ideal is that everything reflect softly, like a CD.

Esther Leslie

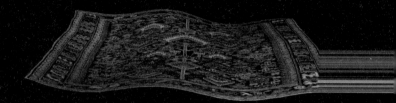

"The player piano was a way of having art without the artist because he's a threat, because the creative artist has to be a threat, so he's swamped by the performer."
William Gaddis

"Dawn is about luminosity and so is the iPad."
David Hockney

A BEAUTIFUL VIRUS INSIDE THE MACHINE:
WILLIAM GADDIS AND *AGAPĒ AGAPE*

The critical and commercial failure in 1955 of William Gaddis's first novel *The Recognitions* necessitated a move into regular employment for the thirty year-old husband and father-to-be. This was the beginning of what would amount to a twenty year stretch writing corporate speeches, articles and film scripts for clients like IBM, Eastman-Kodak and Ford. Gaddis resented what he referred to as "the coffin of the 9-to-5," yet here he was on Wall Street in the midst of post-war America's glorious free market, where winning at business was like winning at baseball, no more than the embodiment of the doctrine of the survival of the fittest. The pretext of 'doing business' in the rush for success sanctioned virtually any act. Kill, or be killed. It's a jungle out there. And so forth. But Gaddis never switched off, he simply suspended his disbelief. Joseph Tabbi has informed us that Gaddis worked by "watching the operations of power, appropriating its language, recycling its massive waste products," and that he proceeded to burrow out and occupy intellectual territory underneath "regimes of information, unreality and bureaucratic domination." As a novelist Gaddis did not hesitate to bite the hand that fed him – an essential quality of any good satirist.

William Gaddis knew he was dying as he wrote *Agapē Agape*, but he made his deadline. The book was completed in 1998 and published in 2002. The allusive title (agapē [from Greek]: selfless, communal love / agape: made into a gap or hole; an expression of shocked disbelief) appropriately suggests a work that encompasses both scholarship and satire. The novella, which has no chapter divisions or even paragraph breaks through its 60 pages, is the frantic monologue of a gravely ill, bed-ridden narrator who has gathered together the multitudinous leaves (no hard drives here) of a lifetime's study of the conquest of technology, made with particular attention to technology's impingement on the role of the artist. As he picks through his papers attempting to edit them into an ordered critique the narrator freely interacts with the abundance of ideas and personalities encompassed by his research. The player piano, as both "a source and an issue of the alienation of skills in work and in leisure," is the fulcrum of this urgent thesis. The novel begins:

"No but you see I've got to explain all this because I don't, we don't know how much time there is left and I have to work on the, to finish this work of mine while I, why I brought in this whole pile of books notes pages clippings and God knows what, get it all organized […] get it cleared up and settled before everything collapses and it's all swallowed up by lawyers and taxes like everything else because that's what it's about, that's what my work is about, the collapse of everything, of meaning, of language, of values, of art, disorder and dislocation wherever you look, entropy drowning everything in sight, entertainment and technology and every four year old with a computer, everybody his own artist where the whole thing comes from, the binary system and the computer where technology came from in the first place, you see?"

By the time of his terminal prognosis in 1997 William Gaddis had accumulated a vast archive of notes and clippings as a result of over half a century of research, which has been described as 'the most penetrating, far-reaching history of the player piano never to be written'. On receiving the news of his illness Gaddis's resolve was invigorated, and he moved to fashion his burgeoning personal studies into publishable form. Gaddis's genius (he officially became a genius in 1982 with a McArthur Award) was to shun drab and emotionless academia and instead deliver his research in the form of an exhilarating work of art, a nail-bomb of dense prose. It's Gaddis as cultural insurgent. *Agapē Agape* was widely ignored upon publication (or erroneously dismissed as an unfinished, posthumous cut and paste job) but ten years on it is more astringent, satirically astute and vital than ever. Through the breathless discourse of his livid narrator Gaddis delivers a vituperative scrutiny of the corruption of artistic values in a world in thrall to technology. He pillories a system so obsessed, as he sees it, by the democratising (read: commercial) potential of mechanisation that it is in danger of eliminating the very creative spring – the people – it depends on. In *Agapē Agape* Gaddis rails against the inexorable creep of 'progress' itself – surely a Canutean enterprise? But perhaps William Gaddis succeeds where Canute is said to have failed. Warren Buffet, our Greatest Living Philanthropist (guilt, perhaps?), corruptly aligned an economic crisis with an uncontrollable force of nature with his Chaunceyism, "It's only when the tide goes out that you learn who's been swimming naked." But, to reclaim the analogy, through Gaddis's sheer craft and conviction *Agapē Agape* forces a dissembling 'sea' of blind acquiescence to progress momentarily and to recede. The naked 'swimmers' are exposed, and Gaddis is standing on the beach with his binoculars.

Born in the 1870s, manufactured, advertised and sold to millions before finally dying "along with everything else in the crash of 1929," the player piano was the disfigured child of an ungainly coupling between art and science – the couple has of course since tied the knot. A contemporary of the more widely (and nostalgically) remembered phonograph, by 1900 the player piano was the leading method of playing back music in the solvent parlours of the day. Tellingly the biggest brand of phonograph, Victrola, purloined its appellation from that of the leading brand of player piano, the Pianola. Originally designed to reproduce popular ditties when pedalled by an operator, the player piano was peddled by buccaneer franchisees using lines (best read aloud in an American accent) such as: "You can play better by roll than many play by hand," and "Now even untrained persons can do it," and "Look Mom, no hands!" Punched paper rolls moved through a mechanism implanted in the instrument that 'read' them and activated the piano's hammers according to the distribution of holes in the roll. Although the costly and bulky player piano finally fell foul of free market 'natural selection', its crude binary technology – the 'survivor gene' – was preserved, inherited and made to evolve. So the player piano – not the phonograph or gramophone – is the true technological predecessor of the CD, MIDI and the mp3, and is likewise the basis for all the digital technology used in modern-day computers.

In *Agapē Agape*, Gaddis, working under the maxim of Know Your Enemy, keenly plots the backstory and legacy of the punched paper technology, revealing its distinguished heritage: the mechanics of Jacques de Vaucanson's automated, shitting duck of the 1740s were based on a punched card system designed to control industrial machinery, a system that was the brainchild of Jean-Baptiste Falcon, the son of – not incidentally – an organist. Vaucanson's duck inspired Joseph-Marie Jacquard's punch-card operated silk looms half a century later, which were widely influential. Then Charles Babbage utilised perforated cards in the design of his 'analytical engine'. Herman Hollerith developed the same concept in the late 19th century and founded the company that would, in 1924, become the International Business Machines Corporation, or IBM. Fast-forward to the IBM stand at 1962's Seattle World Business Fair, and we find an oversized musical box on display that could be hand-cranked by visitors to demonstrate how "stored mathematical information in a modern computer's memory is based on the same general principle as stored musical information in an old-fashioned music box." So the emergence of the player piano in the 1870s marked the point at which a manufacturing technology originally developed from a musical instrument took a 150 year round trip and met itself precisely where it had begun. The irony of this situation was not lost on William Gaddis.

Gaddis's examination of the seep of technology into the arts did not end with the player piano, that is where it began. For Gaddis the player piano was symbolic of a greater malady. It was an iconic instalment in the slip from artistic to entertainment values and a key component, if you will, of the shove to democratise the arts. His complaint stands – even in the light of any number of examples of artists whose work successfully transcended the calculated mimetic functions of their chosen machinery (Lillian Schwartz, Conlon Nancarrow, Kraftwerk…). As Gaddis asserts in *Agapē Agape*, the player piano was the great emblem of "the frenzy of invention and mechanisation and democracy and how to have art without the artist." And yet, under these conditions, "The individual is lost, the unique is lost… authenticity is lost not just authenticity but the whole concept of authenticity." Here is Gaddis's rub. And "Here's Flaubert," invoked on cue by the narrator of *Agapē Agape*, "the entire dream of democracy – to raise the proletariat to the bourgeois level of stupidity."

Stewart Morgan

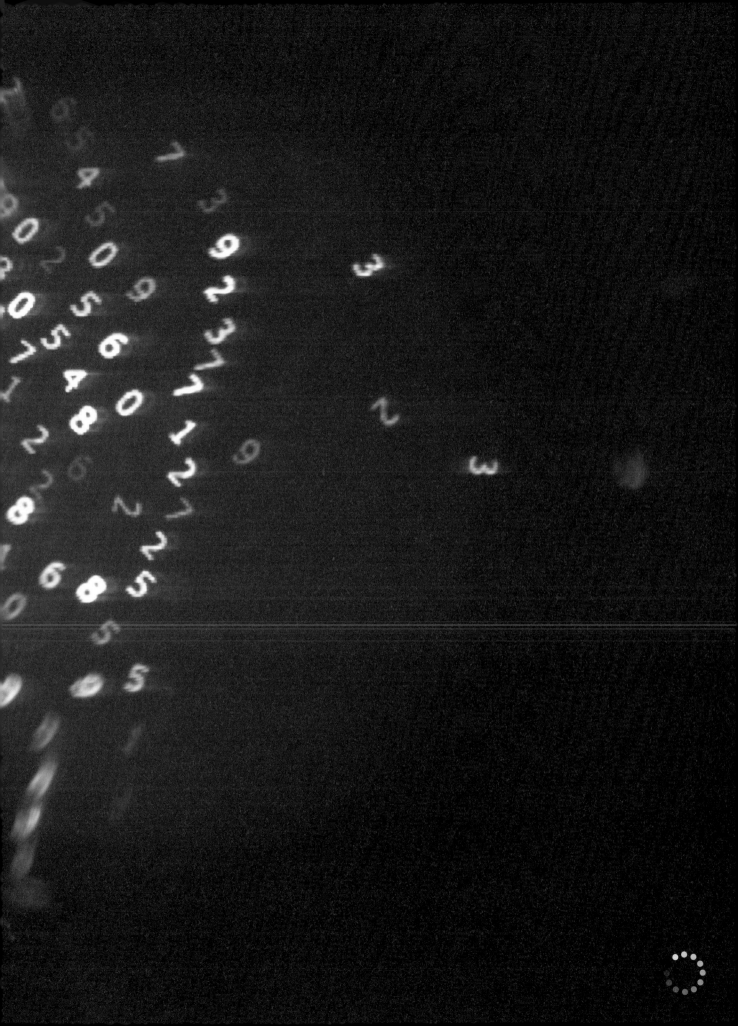

QED

A QR Code (short for Quick Response Code) is the universally acknowledged trademark for a type of matrix barcode (or two-dimensional code). Invented in Japan in 1994, for specialist industrial use, QR codes have become an increasingly prevalent feature of our contemporary mediascape. Their large storage capacity, compared to standard UPC (Universal Product Code) barcodes, and their fast readability, for anyone who owns a smartphone, have contributed to their recent surge in popularity as the latest guiding light (and great white hope) of consumer advertising and packaging.

Where the standard barcode consists of an abstract curtain of minimalist lines fringed by an evenly spaced cluster of digits, the QR code forgoes numbers completely. Deep down, of course, it is *all* numbers – complex, unfolding strings of them, whose repeating patterns of slightly varying permutations are hinted at in the code's intricate pixel patchwork of elementary graphic shapes. If one were to squint, it might almost resemble a fiendish Sudoku or crossword grid, of squares within squares within squares; some of whose spaces have been left deliberately blank, or else have been blacked out in mischief or in pique. Squinting, indeed, may be our instinctive, reflexive response to these Quick Response codes. Hovering at the edge of our vision like the dots of a screen-induced migraine, their bit-mapped blockiness generates the same optical frisson as a Bridget Riley in miniature. Never intended to be easy or pleasing to the human eye, they have been designed to be read by machines.

Take your smartphone out of your pocket, however, and the code is startled into action. Nuzzle your phone up to it, and, as if gazing up through an eyeglass at a particular patch of the sky at night, its fuzzy outline snaps into focus, revealing an unexpected vista, a sense of its hidden depths.

From our vantage point in the present, and with the technology we currently have at our disposal, we may only be getting a small glimpse of what is out there. For all its densely packed nebula of data, the QR code is still only at the trailing edge of a much larger universe.

Yet, like the light of the stars themselves, this apparently trailblazing icon may already be fading at exactly the moment where it has become most clearly visible. Looking forward, we are already projecting far beyond it. Looking back, from that point in the future, the picture that it currently offers may appear to be as crude and simplistic as the view we might have once had with the naked eye.

Steven Bode

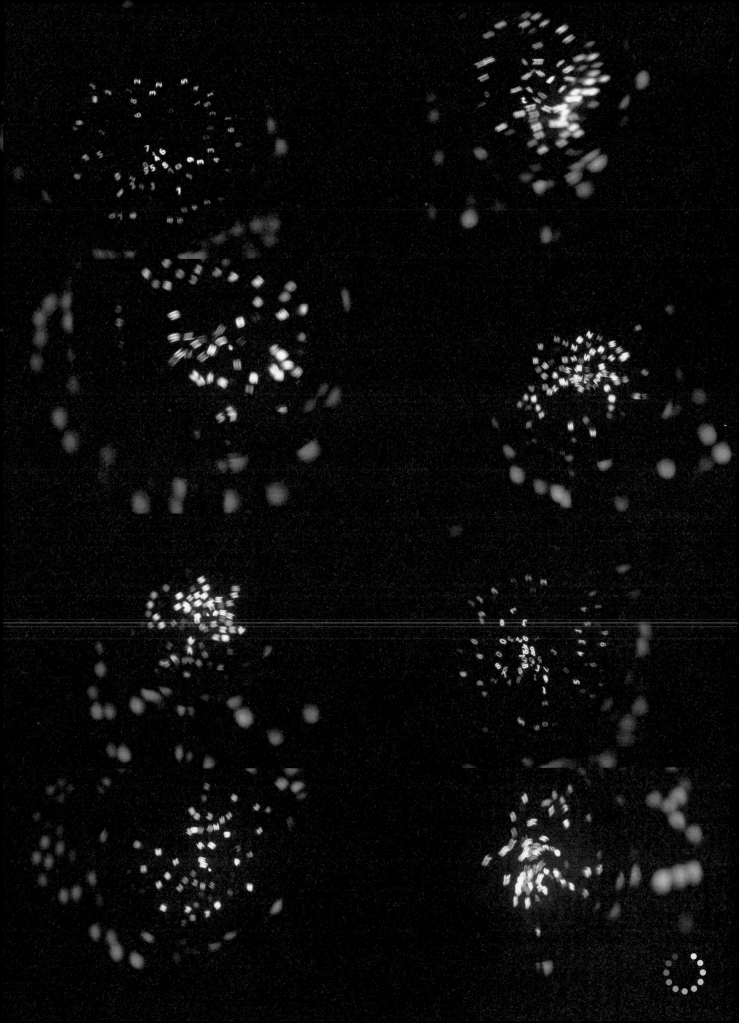

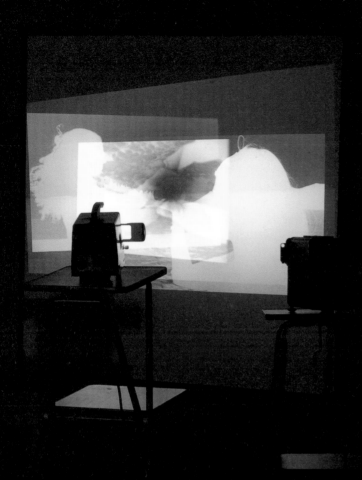

NOISE, LUCK

One day, in the far future, on a faraway moon of a faraway planet, a man discovers what human beings are for. We have been selectively bred to be lucky. The proof is in his own existence: despite all the horrors we have visited on ourselves, he is there, in the far future, on a faraway moon. The only problem left, notes the author of this delightful fable, is that there can be no more stories about a species who is always lucky.

That peripatetic phenomenologist Vilém Flusser had a different theory. We have created a phylum of logical machines capable of anything except randomness. The most reliable random number generators they have access to are human beings. Our function, in the universe of logical machines, is to generate noise. This, he says, is our job: to generate the random for a rational system, and we will keep doing it until, in some final moment of perfection, we have made every image in the galleries of Babel, from the one that is perfect black to the one that is allover white, and every possible image in between. We are functionaries of a machine which is universal in its ambition.

Unfortunately we have, in our own lucky way, become rather good at making the same image over and over again. Thousands upon thousands of sleeping milk-warmed babies, thousands upon thousands of beaches, weddings, parties. Perhaps we are neither so lucky nor so random as might be hoped.

Torsten Lauschmann's *Growing Zeros (Digital Clock)* (2010) might well be the insignia of Flusser's functionaries of the universal machine. No machine is more universal than the clock. We have stood in railway stations and airports watching the steady flack-flack of cleverly assembled mechanical boards and digital displays as they roll over the seconds. In *Growing Zeros* it is as if, as we watch the disembodied hands reposition the component elements of the numerals, we could descry the lineage of ancestors whose patient labours have become entirely automated, assimilated into the logic of ubiquitous digital timepieces. We all serve time in its solemnly inevitable tick and tock; why not show the factory hands whose discipline the clock has enforced with ever more rigour from the hour of clocking-in to the second of counted keystrokes.

In 2011's *Before the Revolution*, machine time takes over perceptual time that in any case was never quick enough. The painted horses leaping over some Victorian racecourse pose in flight like ballerinas, unnatural, as we have learned to say after Muybridge's experimental photography. Until his scientific truth disproved our common knowledge, we thought we could see, only to learn that we were second best to a shutter attached to a length of string. Lauschmann gives us revenge: the icon for an interrupted load spins idly in the middle of the video frame, as if there were more to see of the painting that is already there. The computer strains to complete a motion that will never come to an end. Hahaha you silly computer.

'The machine seems to be an instrument of the mind working against the body' runs a moment of voiceover in *Misshapen Pearl*, a video reflection on Flusser's reflections on the invisibility of streetlamps. Flusser is unsure: is the mind the sickness of the body, or the body the sickness of the mind? The problem, in Flusser voiced by Lauschmann, is that humanity is divided from the primate only by culture, but in our denatured state, culture is our nature. Flusser was not the first or last but a poet among those philosophers who have thought, from Marx to Stiegler, about the fit of human, nature and technology. They do not fit. Three torn parts of an integral whole to which they do not add up.

The primate sits, bewildered, perhaps, on the pianola under the snow in the spotlight of *The Coy Lover*, a toy. The pianola is a toy. Even when it is a Disklavier and programmed through software, a toy. Culture is the set of toys we play with to keep the dark at bay. *Lares et penates*. Not just any toys, though: think of the ghostly plethora of inhuman music in Conlan Nancarrow's compositions cut directly into piano rolls; or of the uncanny moment in Renoir's *La Règle du Jeu* when the pianist watches the keyboard play the danse macabre. Impossibly wet, the snow drifts down, announced by a mechanical whirr, and out of darkness the notes tumble over one another, flakes of sound crystallised out of white noise, and you wonder idly if the water will fuse the electrics. Nature is always with us, the gorilla on the piano, bamboozled. And we are always there, the pianist who fails to turn up to play the cultural rhapsody that continues without us playing a note.

The interweaving intricacies of humans and technologies are not a theme in Lauschmann but a condition. There is no transmission without static, no reason without contingency, no thing without stuff. Everything depends on everything else: numbers, coincidences, the flight of starlings. *Dear Scientist, Please Paint Me* (2011) says it exactly. We seek the expert ratification that would prove, as Muybridge disproved, our existence and our own precious claims to know, to know knowledge at least, even if we have to sign truth off to another department. An aurora borealis on the gallery walls, accompanied by a soundtrack which seems less music than sonics designed to explain the acoustic space of the gallery, light soaking into the luminous paint, more where the lamp pauses, less where it slips across space. The solar storms that drive static in the radio frequencies drive the polar auroras, but it is a program that drives this, as also many other works, described by the artist as 'control software'.

Had we but world enough and time… In Marvell's poem it was the mistress who was coy: in Lauschmann it is the lover, bashfully approaching those bodies that have become unnatural, in daytime rooms plunged into dark, with false suns made of headlamps and hanging lenses, where numbers and other glitches break up the seamless cloth of the technical phylum, and through it, like clockwork monkeys banging on our drums, programmed but random, tragically lucky, we blunder coyly, from far futures and faraway worlds towards the place we must always stand, underneath the streetlight, looking for the stars.

Sean Cubitt

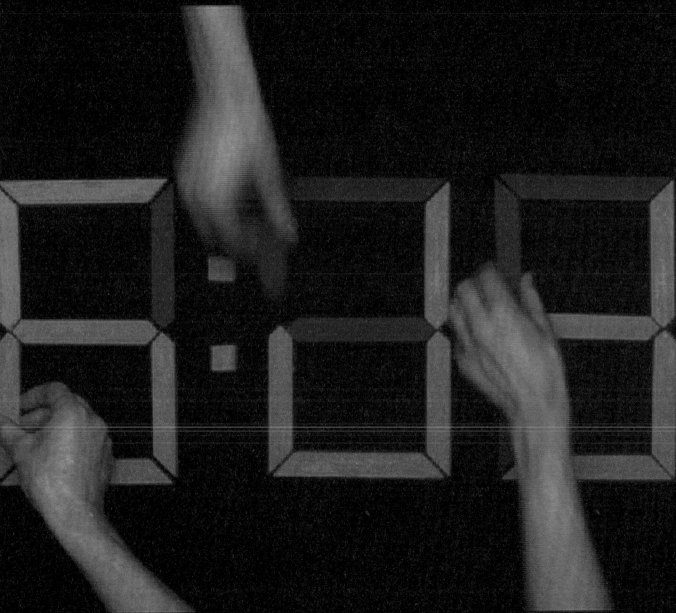

THIS PAGE INTENTIONALLY LEFT BLANK

When the pianola plays and the snow falls, the projection screen is intentionally left blank.

When the five slide projectors shine an image, the pianola and the snow machine are intentionally left blank.

When the luminous wall is drawn upon by the roving light, the screen, the pianola and the snow machine are intentionally left blank.

The conceit is that the snow from the snow machine plays the tune on the pianola and in so doing prompts the light to come on in a Fischli/Weiss *the way things go* cause and effect kind of way.

Sun For Five Nights sees five solarised images projected from different angles that converge at the point of common concern – a protagonist reaching for or catching the sun. The solarisation makes the sun appear black – no longer the emanatory source of light. The work calls to mind the pseudo-science fiction short film *La Jetée* by Chris Marker (1962) that is made up almost entirely from photographic slides and a future/past world loops.

And it also drives the patterns appearing as *Dear Scientist, Please Paint Me* which consists of luminous paint, a moving headlight, controlling software and a moving and participant audience. It is an equivalent and a neat homage to Kippenberger's *Dear Painter, Paint for Me* but the instruction is to science. The unknowable blankness of Dark Matter has been troubling scientists who need to label or explain everything. Astronomers have come to think of luminous galaxies as mere bright flecks embedded in a halo of dark material. And this is why an intentionally left blank page is left blank.

Graham Domke

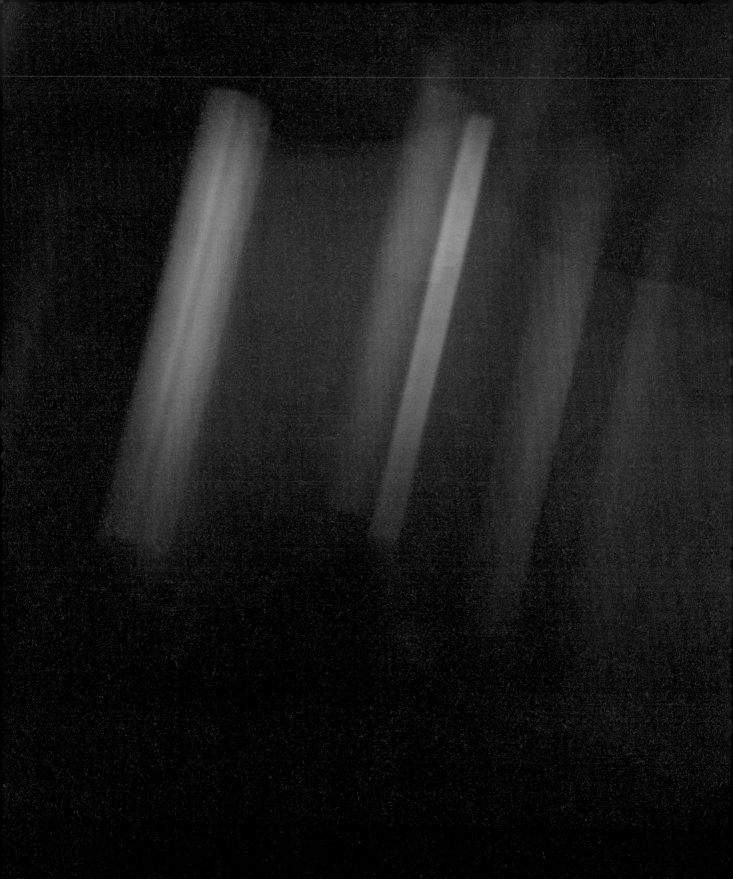

LUMINESCENCE

Screens always glow. Screens are luminous. Luminescence is a slight thing, a barely present thereness of light, a tinge of colour. Insubstantial it may be, but luminosity is the stuff or non-stuff of film. The luminescence makes the artificial world of the screen a place of eye-catching delight. This radiance turns into our own bio-luminescence, as we stay for an hour or so, bathed in that light. Radiance pervades our liquid crystallised, digital environment today, as, through the ubiquity of the liquid crystal, it makes itself more and more at home in our every device, from mobile phones to TVs, to PCs to home cinema and data projectors. It is no surprise that the super-robots of anime, such as Mazinger Z, fire photonic beams from their eyes – in so doing, they collapse their own bio-luminescent functioning onto the mechanism of anime itself. The luminous jungle in Studio Ghibli's *Nausicaa* was, when drawn in 1984, a vision of a futurity then still to come. We inhabit it fully now. And yet phosphor-fluorescence remains a signal of something odd, unknown, future-oriented, because its hues do not seem to be contained in the rainbow, but are rather a property of our machines and laboratories or something seemingly utterly alien to us. Seemingly, for, in fact, that glaucous light shares something with the glow seen on the disturbed surface of the oceans from which we all once long ago stemmed. Fluorescence is a marginal, maligned, curious, questionable phenomenon, but a persistent one. It flashes into the culture and disappears again regularly. Periodically a fashion for neon clothing or nail varnish cycles round again. Fluorescence as a quality of light plus colour has a bad reputation in many contexts – associated with the cheap, the vulgar, the garish, and the artificial, as opposed to the authentic, valid, stylish, elegant. Fluorescence, certainly as it applies to colours, has so often signified something that is suspect, overly intense, off-colours, odd colours, wrong colours, chemical tints. Fluorescent colours – colours that shine too brightly, too

intensely, colours that warp the prism, violate the rainbow and shatter the spectrum. These are colours from somewhere else – some only glimpsed in dreams or grotesque visions, some educed in the imagination, some cooked up in the laboratory to outdo the natural world. In the mid-nineteenth century, phosphorescence was the quality that drew approbation. It was a term for something worthless, foolish, rubbish, empty talk, nonsense such that Thomas Carlyle could speak of 'phosphorescent punk and nothingness'. Phosphorescent punk was killing the popular mind and was the sum total of weak novels, poor humour, bad poetry, skim-milk history and diluted science. Phosphorescence featured in Carlyle's favourite insult and it referred to a quality of putrid fermentation, the turbulent senseless activity of rot, decay, bacteria. For Walter Benjamin phosphorescent light is always associated with decay, for it is, unlike the fluorescent, an emission that stores up energy and then releases it slowly, decaying, weakening over time. Furthermore, it arises when rot sets in. In his study of Baroque mourning plays, Benjamin associates it not with the bright happy luminosity of Enlightenment, but with a non-brightening glimmer from the depths of the earth. He writes:

If the lesson of Socrates, that knowledge of good makes for good actions, may be wrong, this is far more true of knowledge about evil. And it is not as an inner light, a lumen naturale, that this knowledge shines forth in the night of mournfulness, but a subterranean phosphorescence glimmers from the depths of the earth. It kindles the rebellious, penetrating gaze of Satan in the contemplative man.

Benjamin devoted a file of the *Arcades Project* to 'Modes of Lighting'. He wanted to align types of light and social significance. And in his own period he recognises the absolute force of the new neon lights of the city, asking:

What, in the end, makes advertisements so superior to criticism?
Not what the moving red neon sign says – but the fiery pool
reflecting it in the asphalt.

The commodity's name and logo is of less importance than the
migration of the sign across space, its descent into the streets, its
excessiveness that makes it leap outside itself – 'hits us between
the eyes', in anticipation of what Day-Glo Color Corp come to
call 'higher impact'. It 'hurls things at us', notes Benjamin, into our
path, transforming the blackness of the road into mythic blazing
dancing necromantic swirls. Benjamin describes through this light,
through this advertising, through this self-display of the commodity,
animated vision – mobile products, anthropomorphised nature.
When it came to latter-day future dreams for colour schemes, Punk
preferred fluorescence's immediate shock of the glow in the dark
and the glow by day to phosphorescence's postponed illumination
of its own self in the darkness. In Punk, fluorescence found a
place, in its vaunting of anti-nature, of garish offensiveness, an
embrace of it all its vulgar connotations and all its power to shock
and surprise. Fluorescence holds nothing back for later, its mode is
the mode of anti-interiority, denial of romantic self, a cheap trick, a
cheap trip without innerness, an upfront slap in the face of public
taste. The chief designer of the look was Jamie Reid. In the early
1970s Reid, influenced by Situationist theories of detournement
and occupying enemy forms, designed and distributed some
fluorescent stickers with slogans like 'Save Petrol – Burn Cars'
and 'Special Offer – This shop welcomes shoplifters'.

Esther Leslie

I have been told that there was a time when privileged men and women climbed church towers to look at a invention they called horizon. It was glorious. They decended with the vision of a new invention: The Panorama, 360° of continues walls for the masses. Containment and Protection, resistance and refuge. Cheap tickets for children and Soldiers.
Fast forward. Movement can only be represented by movement. By reducing the picture to a film frame the individual image subordinate itself to velocity. 24 times in a second, 1440 times in a minute, 2073600 times in a day the hidden meaning of individuality is overlooked by the gasping eye.

The devil, oblong in shape, sixteen by nine to be exact, creates global confidence with international standards. Silver and white, punctured for God's penetrating and sychronised voice, he mirrors our lack of empathy. Off-screen is where he can't hide.

I am tired, I want to show what is behind and above. I want to stand tall, look at it.
The streetlamps, cars, hedges & birds in their uncompressed glory. Life in low resolution without a start and end. A long fade follows a long fade. Troths which no longer entertain become lies.
I can hear Pinochio saying: "my nose will be growing!"

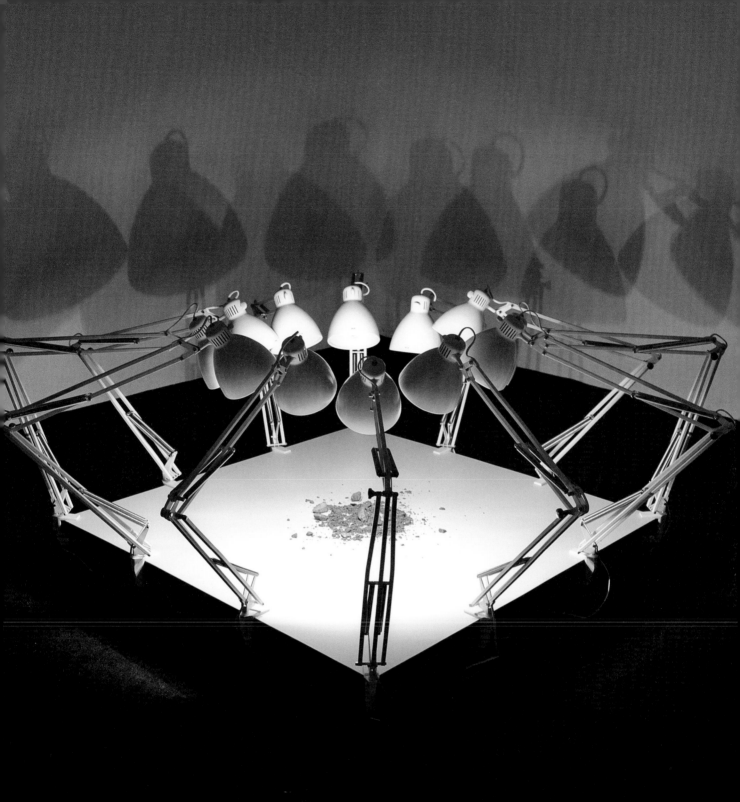

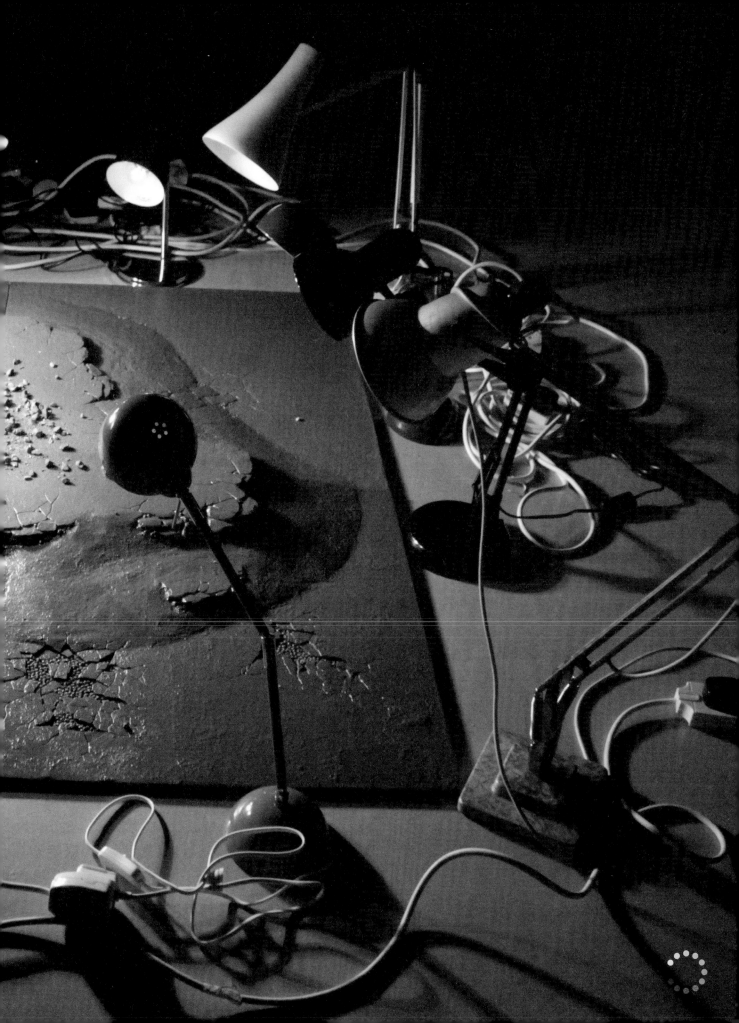

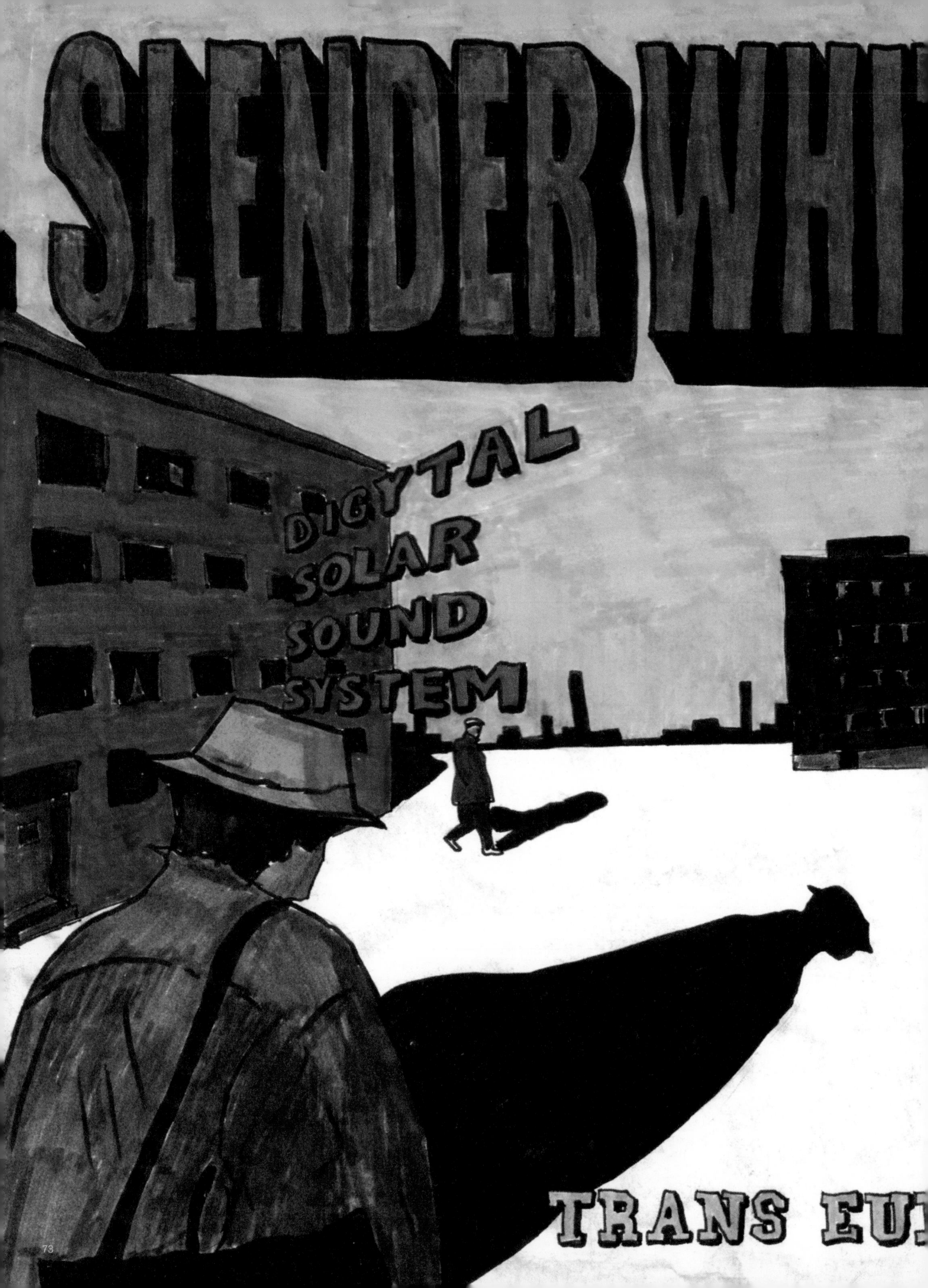
SLENDER WHI
DIGYTAL
SOLAR
SOUND
SYSTEM
TRANS EU

would not be proceeded against, and a number of them accordingly did so, M.H. apparently amongst them. M.H.'s brother got off at this time, but they 'put him away', a euphemism apparently for Van Diemen's Land. This brother wrote the song which I enclose, and as M.H. 'has had many a pot of beer for singing it', he probably has given it me pretty correctly…

The Owslebury Lads [51]

On the thirtieth of November last, Eighteen hundred and thirty,
Our Owslebury lads they did prepare,all for the machinery,
And when they did get there, My eye! How they let fly;
The machinery fell to pieces in the twinkling of an eye.

[Chorus:]
Oh! Mob, such a mob never was seen before,
And if we live this hundred years we never shall no more.

FLURRY

Snow globes, like toys or children's books – all objects that are trivial, each one a spike of imagination and longing – present themselves, to use Benjamin's methodological term, as 'dialectical images', points of stilled focus in which the historical relations of life might be made visible, or, to use another of Benjamin's terms, they encourage the concoction of 'dialectics at a standstill'. This is a temporary freezing of the flux of time – exercised on an image or object – for purposes of analysis. And, conversely, it is the moving into flux of frozen (in Lukacs' terms, reified) relations – the production of links between things, parts, moments. Flurry and freeze could be seen as codes for the subjective and the objective, so neatly kept apart in social theory. Flurry as subjective blur. Freeze as the cool eye that apprehends a deadened scene. Through Benjamin, it is possible to arrive at a method, a mode of analysing phenomena that refuses conventional distinctions between 'objectivity' and 'subjectivity', and that constantly evokes both freeze and flurry as necessary aspects of knowing. Perhaps the snow globe, in particular, engages these dual forces of flux and freezing intimate to Benjamin's modernity and methodology: intermittently, when a snow globe is grabbed, a moment of quake or shattering – Erschütterung – is enacted. Such shattering is vaunted by Benjamin in his 1930s essay *The Work of Art in the Age of its Technical Reproducibility* in relation to a reformulation of aesthetic forms, characterised as the 'liquidation of the traditional value of the cultural heritage' brought about by film, photography and reproducible art forms. The drama of flux and flurry inside the snow globe provides a dialectical image. The snow globe's flurry of artificial snow shatters the contemplative status quo, proposing both epistemological confusion and the transformative power of action. Simultaneously, the globe condenses a frozen scene, a moment in time – however idealised – isolated for critical appropriation.

Taking snow globes seriously? The snow globe, by most accounts, an object of kitsch delight, of banalised Romantic reverie, became controversial in 2006, when it was placed on the list of banned items in carry on luggage on US aeroplanes. On the US Transport Security Administration website snow globes were cited under other prohibited objects: 'Snow globes and like decorations regardless of size or amount of liquid inside, even with documentation'. Indeed one online commentator mocked the security paranoia as 'a global war on snow globes'. Such a war sounds ridiculous because of the triviality of the snow shaker as object. It gains particular frisson, though, because war is declared on something designed to present a scene of contemplative tranquility, an encapsulation of the dreamy desire for harmony and peace on an Earth where all clamour is muffled and all darkness expunged by the gently falling snow dust.

To find terror inside a snow globe is, oddly, to return to it the force of the now downgraded Romantic aesthetic from which it drew and which it tamed. The snow globe – as landscape scene – contained and domesticated the extremities of climate and nature that evoked sublime affect. Edmund Burke and Immanuel Kant characterised sublime experience in relation to dramatic visions of a boiling, raging sea or claps of thunder and lightning flashes, howling storms and sudden avalanches. These elements found their own containment in aesthetic form in images such as JMW Turner's *Snow Storm – Steam Boat off a Harbour's Mouth*, from 1842. Kant's sublime, a self-shattering affect, was evoked in the viewer by the awful shudders of earthquake or the sight of the mass of shapeless mountain masses piled on one another in wild disarray, with their pyramids of ice, or the turbulence of the gloomy raging sea. For Kant, beauty and the sublime are differentiated in

relation to form. Beauty 'is connected with the form of the object'.
The object has definable 'boundaries', while the sublime 'is to be
found in a formless object', represented by a 'boundlessness'.
Wild, eruptive nature – the swirling sea, massive ice floes, a
looming, dark, snow-capped mountain, a churning ice storm, a
sudden chasm – provokes in the viewer a welter of feelings, but
most notably a type of terror as the mind realises the immensity
and indifference to humanity of that which is perceived. The mind
struggles to regain its composure and superiority to blind nature.
Terror bursts out of nature. Now terror, largely fantasmatic, bursts
out of snow globes.

Esther Leslie

LIST OF WORKS

Cover, foldout & page 1
*Skipping Over Damaged
Areas,* 2010
Single screen HD video, 10 mins
Commissioned by Lux
Photo: TL

Page 3–8
Byt, 2011/12
Oak shelf, objects, video
projection, 6mins (looped)
DCA, Dundee
Supported by DCA and
Film and Video Umbrella
Photos: Ruth Clark, TL/DB

Page 9–14
The Coy Lover, 2011 (2012)
Yamaha Disklavier, snow machine,
control soft and hardware, 16mm
projector/moving head light
DCA, Dundee
Laing Gallery, Newcastle
(AV 12 Festival),
John Hansard Gallery, Southampton
Commissioned by DCA
Photos: Ruth Clark, Steve Shrimpton

Page 17–20
Stuntmen with Skirts, 2010 (2011/12)
HD video, monitor, 2 min (looped)
DCA, Dundee
Supported by Collective
Gallery, Edinburgh
Photos: Ruth Clark, TL

Page 21–26, 45
Fathers Monocle, 2011/12
Video projection, meniscus
lens, lens holder, motor, custom
game engine
Commissioned by Film and
Video Umbrella
DCA, Dundee
Laing Gallery, Newcastle
(AV 12 Festival)
John Hansard Gallery, Southampton
Photos: Ruth Clark, Steve Shrimpton,
Zoha Zokaei, TL

Page 27–34
Sun For Five Nights, 2011/12
Single slide projectors, 35mm
slides, luminous wall/screen,
control soft and hardware,
speakers / Yamaha Disklavier
DCA, Dundee
Laing Gallery, Newcastle
(AV 12 Festival)
John Hansard Gallery, Southampton
Supported by DCA
Photos: Ruth Clark, Steve Shrimpton,
TL/DB

Page 35–37
House of the Rising Sun, 2009
Wall painting, video projection,
3 mins (looped)
DCA, Dundee
Photos: Ruth Clark, TL

Page 39–44
Digital Clock (Growing Zeros), 2010
HD video projection/monitor,
dimensions variable, 24 hour (looped)
Glasgow International 2010
Collective Gallery, Edinburgh
DCA, Dundee
Kunsthalle, Hamburg
BBC Screen, Bradford
Photos: Ruth Clark, TL

Page 46–54
Dear Scientist, Please Paint Me, 2011
Luminous paint, DMX controlled
moving head light, speakers
DCA, Dundee
Commissioned by DCA
Supported by Creative Scotland
Photos: Ruth Clark

Page 55, 56
Dead Man's Switch, 2008
HD video projection, gallery
lighting control hard and software,
5 mins (looped)
ICA, London
Photos: ICA, TL

Page 57, 58, 60
*Truths which no longer entertain
become lies,* 2011/12
Video projector, media player,
window, 4 mins (looped), sound
DCA, Dundee
Supported by DCA
Photos: Ruth Clark, TL/DB

Page 59, 61, 62
Before the Revolution, 2011
Monitor, media player, video,
2 mins (looped)
DCA, Dundee
John Hansard Gallery, Southampton
Supported by DCA
Photos: Ruth Clark, Steve Shrimpton

Page 63–64
Lifelike, 2008 (2012),
12 luxo desktop lamps, DMX light
controller, table, stones, soil
Edith Russ Haus, Oldenburg
Supported by Edith Russ Haus
Photo: Sam Luntley, Katja Giersig

Page 65–68
Lifelike, 2008 (2012),
12 used desktop lamps, DMX
light controller, battle game board,
stones, sand
John Hansard Gallery, Southampton
Photos: Steve Shrimpton, TL

Page 69–72
Lifelike, 2008 (2009)
24 stage lights, DMX light
controller, stage rigging, grass
and leaves
Scottish National Galleries,
Edinburgh
Photos: TL

Page 73–76
Slender Whiteman, Trans Europe Busking Tour, since 2002
Solar-powered laptop busking sound system
Various countries and online
www.slenderwhiteman.com

Page 77–80
Sequencer (Inconsistent Whisper), 2012
Performance with Red Note Ensemble and Friends
Premiered on 07/04/2012 at The Arches Theater, Glasgow, as part of Behaviour & Counterflow Festival
Commissioned by Red Note Ensemble
Photos: Laurie Irvine

Page 15, 81, 82
At the heart of everything a row of holes, 2011
National Theater St Kilda, Melbourne
Commissioned by 2011 Glasgow Film Festival
Supported by Creative Scotland
Photos: TL

Page 93–96
9 to 5, 2012
Microphones, stands, DMX controlled moving head light, video and slide projection, sound
John Hansard Gallery, Southampton
Photos: Steve Shrimpton, TL

Page 99, 100
Growing Zeros, 2008 (2011)
24 hour (looped), video projection
Ratio3, San Francisco
Photos: TL

Page 103–104
Piecework Orchestra, 2007
40 household machines, control soft and hardware
Norwegian Church, Swansea
Commissioned by Locws
Photos: Locws

THUMBNAILS

Page 89 (left to right)
Places of Exposure, 1997
Framed photograph
Mackintosh Gallery, Glasgow

Ferral, 2010
Video projection, 2 mins (looped)
ICA, London

He got the whole world in his hand, 2009
Sound sculpture, 4 mins (looped)
Mary Mary, Glasgow

At the heart of everything a row of holes, 2011 (2012)
Expanded cinema projection
Melbourne

The Curtain, 2006 (2007)
Converted shop unit with real time video projection
Contemporary Art Norwich

Page 90
The dust has come to stay, 2004
Video projection on wall painting and objects
Independent Studios, Glasgow

Marcel, 2006
Ink on printed paper
Mary Mary, Glasgow

Reduced Landscape, 1999
Framed photograph
British Council, Edinburgh

The Mathematician, 2006
Video installation
Mary Mary, Glasgow

Joy Ride, 2009
Slide projection
Mary Mary, Glasgow

Suburbia in 3D, 2004
Video projection on wall painting
Transmission Gallery, Glasgow

Interference Even, 2009
Video projection, 4 mins (looped)
Mary Mary, Glasgow

Page 91
Rope Dancing, 2006
Video projection
GI 2006, Glasgow

Installation, 2006
Mary Mary, Glasgow

Places of Exposure, 1997
Framed photograph
Mackintosh Gallery, Glasgow

Torsten, 2004
Video installation
Transmission Gallery, Glasgow

Perpetual Adoration, 2009
Slide projection
Mary Mary, Glasgow

Sequencer (Inconsistent Whisper), 2012
Performance
Arches, Glasgow

Pandora's Ball, 2008
Video installation
Gallery of Modern Art, Glasgow

Page 92
Hot, hot, cold, hot, 2006 (2008)
Kinetic sculpture
Arnolfini, Bristol

Places of Exposure, 1997
Framed photograph
Mackintosh Gallery, Glasgow

Dear Scientist, Please Paint Me, 2011/12
DCA, Dundee

Places of Exposure, 1997
Framed photograph
Mackintosh Gallery, Glasgow

House of the rising sun, 2009 (2011)
Video projection on wall painting
Gallery One, Bradford

The Curtain, 2006
Real time Video Projection
Tramway, Glasgow

Page 97
Money Chord, 2008 (2012)
Video projection, organ, bank notes
West Gallery, Dan Haag

Places of Exposure, 1997
Framed photograph
Mackintosh Gallery, Glasgow

At the heart of everything a row of holes, 2011

Expanded cinema projection
GFT, Glasgow

Misshapen Pearl, 2003
Film still
Venice Bienalle

Sketch for Skipping over damaged areas, 2010

Reduced Landscape, 1999
Framed photograph
British Council, Edinburgh

Photograph, 2009
Glasgow

Event Invite, 2000
Menagerie, Belfast

Page 98
Glasgow, 2006
Stuffed peacock, brown paper, paint
Mary Mary, Glasgow

Wunst, 2004
Participation performance
Transmission Gallery, Glasgow

Mother and Child, 2004
Video projection on gold paint
Transmission Gallery, Glasgow

Surrender, 2006
Video projection on wall painting
GI 2006, Glasgow

Fear among scientists, 2008
Sculpture and wall painting
Gallery of Modern Art, Glasgow

Cold Water Quartet, 2003 – 2005
Audio-visual live performance with 3 Goldfish
ICA, London

Places of Exposure, 1997
Framed photograph
Mackintosh Gallery, Glasgow

Joy Ride, 2009
Slide projection
Mary Mary, Glasgow

Page 101
It all gone tits up again, 2010
Parking sign, camera obscura
Collective Gallery

Me as a fully functioning microphone, 2005
Halloween, somewhere in Glasgow
SAD, 2012
Slide projection
John Hansard Gallery, Southampton

The Coy Lover, 2001 (2012)
Installation
Laing Gallery, Newcastle

Birdmachine, 2012
Sound sculpture
John Hansard Gallery, Southampton

The Coy Lover, 2011 (2012)
Installation
John Hansard Gallery, Southampton

Torsten Lauschmann, 2012
Installation
John Hansard Gallery, Southampton

Piecework Orchestra (Detail), 2007
Performance with 40 household machines
National Waterfront Museum, Swansea

Page 102
The Disillusionist, 2009
Slide projection
Mary Mary, Glasgow

The Coy Lover (detail), 2011 (2012)
Installation
Laing Gallery, Newcastle

Polaroid, 2006
The Modern Institute, Glasgow

Photograph, 2011
DCA, Dundee

Skipping over damaged areas, 2010 (2011/12)
DCA, Dundee

Wrong life cant be lived rightly, 2009
Slide projection
Mary Mary, Glasgow

Exhibition Invite, 2009
Gallery of Modern Art, Glasgow

Piecework Orchestra, 2007
Performance with 40 household machines
National Waterfront Museum, Swansea

RIO CINEMA
FRIDAY 14 OCT

TYRANNOSAUR [18]

2 15

6 45

SLEEPING BEAUTY [18]

4 30

9 00

TORSTEN LAUSCHMANN
EVENT

12 MIDNIGHT

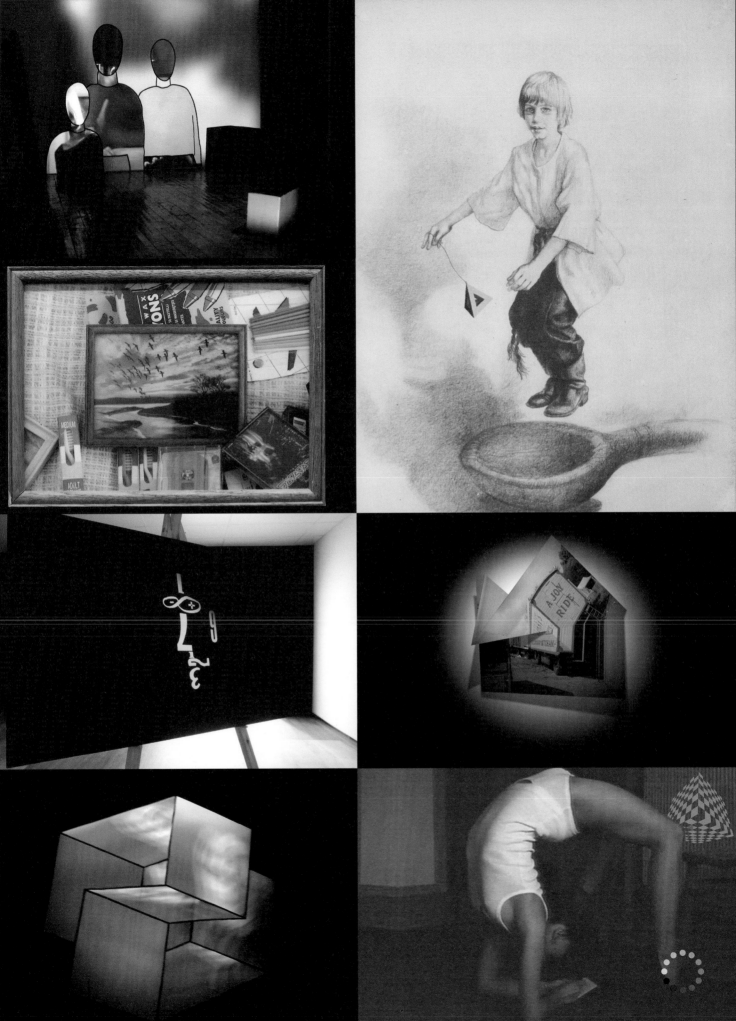

TORSTEN LAUSCHMANN

4 experimental shortfilms

+ Records from the golden age
of Electronic Music

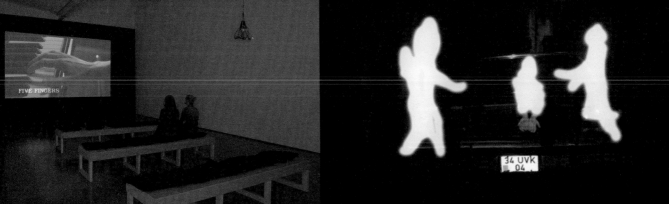

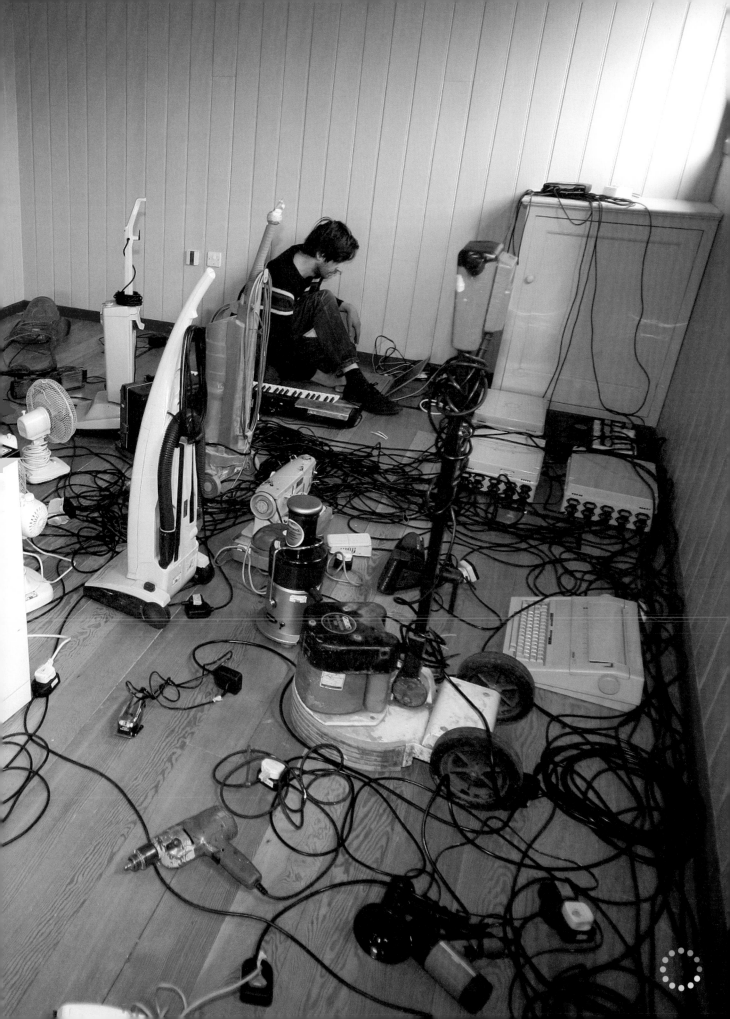

Many thanks to Graham Domke for inviting me to exhibit at Dundee Contemporary Arts and for the support throughout the project. Further thanks to Steven Bode & Film and Video Umbrella for supporting the exhibitions, publication and app. I would like to also thank Creative Scotland, AV Festival, Laing Gallery, John Hansard Gallery & all the other venues featured in this publication. A special thanks goes to Esther Leslie, Sean Cubitt, Stewart Morgan, Clive Gillman, Ewan Wilson, Iain Pate, Rebecca Shatwell, Steven Legget, Ros Carter, Julian Grater, Stephen Foster, Heather Corcoran, Mike Jones, Sam & Anna Luntley, Richy Lamb, Alex Shaw, Ruth Clark, Lucy Richards, Laurie Irvine, Red Note Ensemble, Mum, Dad, Cathy, Hans, Joy and everyone who worked on the installation teams. Finally I would like to thank David Bellingham for his clarity, enthusiasm and patience in editing this book with me.

Torsten Lauschmann
www.lauschmann.com

This publication has been produced to accompany the exhibition *Startle Reaction* at Dundee Contemporary Arts in association with Film and Video Umbrella. Works from this exhibition were subsequently presented at AV Festival 12 and John Hansard Gallery. *Startle* is the first monograph dedicated to Torsten Lauschmann's engaging and multifaceted practice. It looks beyond these exhibitions to celebrate an artistic imagination whose inventive embrace of new (and old) technology offers both a spotlight on the past and an intriguing glimpse into the future. It is entirely fitting therefore that there is a Lauschmann app to go alongside the book.

Graham Domke, Exhibitions Curator Dundee Contemporary Arts
Steven Bode, Director Film and Video Umbrella

Published by Dundee Contemporary Arts & Film and Video Umbrella

Edited by Torsten Lauschmann and David Bellingham

Lauschmann app commissioned by Film and Video Umbrella

Photography by Ruth Clark, Torsten Lauschmann, Sam Luntley, Katja Giersig, David Bellingham, Steve Shrimpton and Zoha Zokaei

Designed by Richy Lamb, Owned and Operated
Distributed by Art Data, www.artdata.co.uk

ISBN 978-0-9558769-5-0

Dundee Contemporary Arts
152 Nethergate
Dundee DD1 4DY
—
www.dca.org.uk

Film and Video Umbrella
8 Vine Yard
London SE1 1QL
—
www.fvu.co.uk

22 October, 2011 – 8 January, 2012
Dundee Contemporary Arts
Dundee

—

1 March – 6 May, 2012
AV Festival 12
Laing Gallery
Newcastle

—

26 June – 11 August, 2012
John Hansard Gallery
Southampton

DCA
Dundee Contemporary Arts

Film and Video
Umbrella

 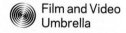 ARTS COUNCIL ENGLAND LOTTERY FUNDED  DISCOVERY FILM FESTIVAL

Last Embrace

KIND
LADY

SABRINA

THE AWAKENING

BAD DREAMS

AWAKE

in
Shock

TERRIFIED

Alice
Sweet
alice

"Best Friends"

THE HAPPENING

ADOLPH ZUKOR PRESENTS
CAROLE
LOMBARD AND FRED MacMURRAY
in
HANDS ACROSS the TABLE
WITH
Ralph Bellamy · Astrid Allwyn
Ruth Donnelly · Marie Prevost
COPYRIGHT MCMXXXV by PARAMOUNT PRODUCTIONS, INC.
ALL RIGHTS RESERVED

er

The
Hand

DEAD MEAT

AND
NOW THE
SCREAMING STARTS

DAVID CRONENBERG'S
THE
BROOD

in
Ball
of
Fire

SHE

PROFONDO
ROSSO

BLOOD

BLOOD ON
SATAN'S CLAW
© Tigon British Film Productions Ltd. and Chilton Film and
Television Enterprises Ltd.
MCMLXX All Rights Reserved

SHE

皇家女將
SHE SHOOTS STRAIGHT

The Hand

HER BEST MOVE

RED &
SHE CAME FROM BEHIND
MUCKY

THE
BEAST

GOTCHA!

THE
BEAST MUST DIE

SABRINA

THE
THING

THE SURVIVOR
Copyright © MCMLXXX RIACI INVESTMENTS PTY. LTD.
All rights reserved under international conventions.

ATTACK OF THE
CRAB
MONSTERS

ATTACK
OF THE
GIANT LEECHE

ATTACK
OF THE KILLER
TOMATOES!

IN THE JOHN HEYMAN PRODUCTION
OF JOSEPH LOSEY'S
BOOM

IRVING STONE'S
The
Agony and the Ecstasy

Sabrina
The Animated Series

THE BIG MAN

BOUNCE